HOW DOES YOUR BONKERS BRAIN WORK?

Written by John Farndon
Illustrated by Alan Rowe

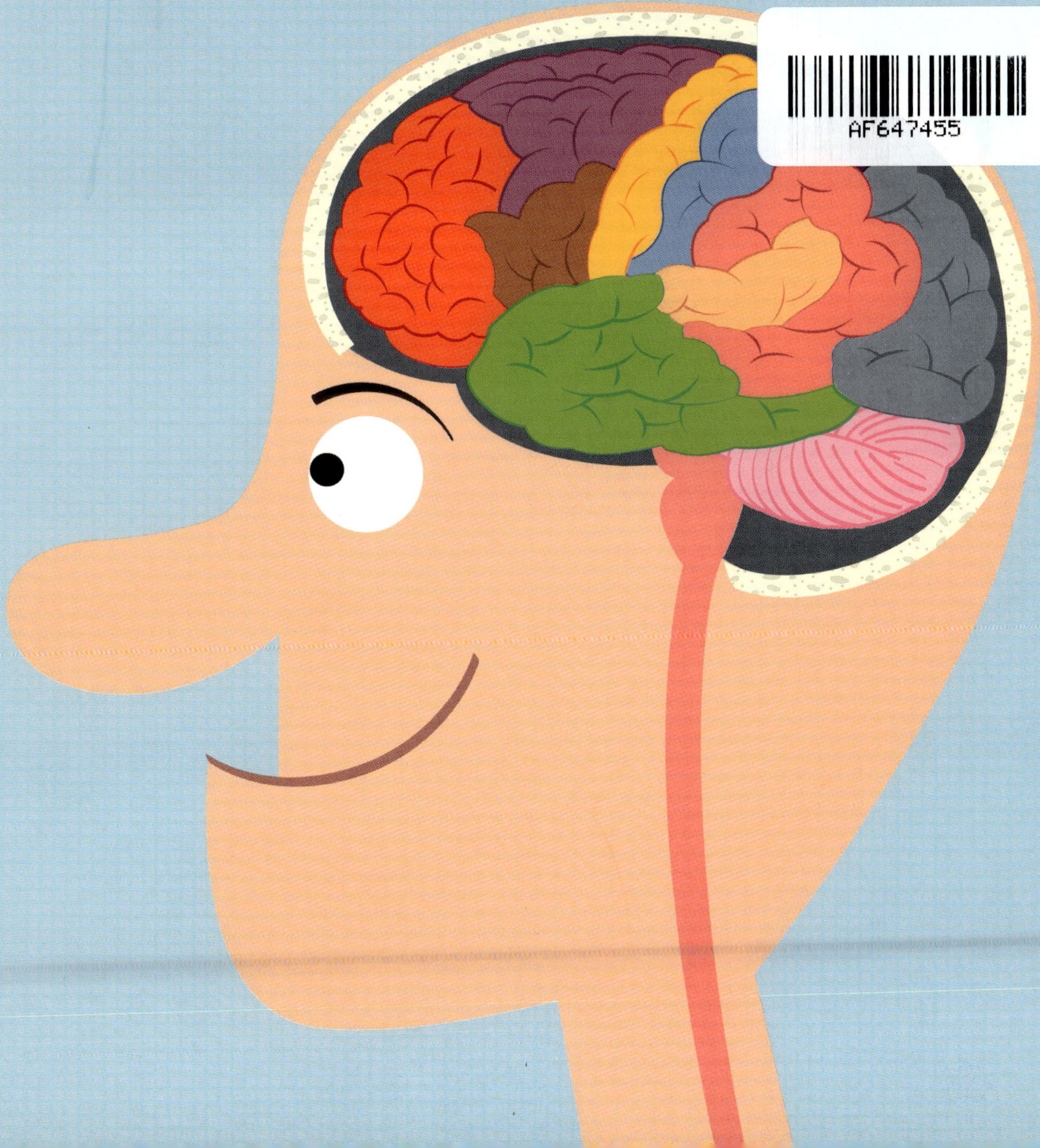

First published in 2023 by Hungry Tomato Ltd
F15, Old Bakery Studios, Blewetts Wharf, Malpas Road, Truro, Cornwall, TR1 1QH, UK.

A CIP catalogue record for this book is available from the British Library.

Published and Distributed in India by Scholastic India Pvt. Ltd.

ISBN 978-93-5954-268-3

This reprint edition : January 2025

Printed in India at Shree Maitrey Printech Pvt. Ltd., Noida

Discover more at
www.hungrytomato.com

CONTENTS

HOW DOES YOUR BRAIN WORK?

Your body is an incredible machine that can do all sorts of amazing things, and your brain controls it all!

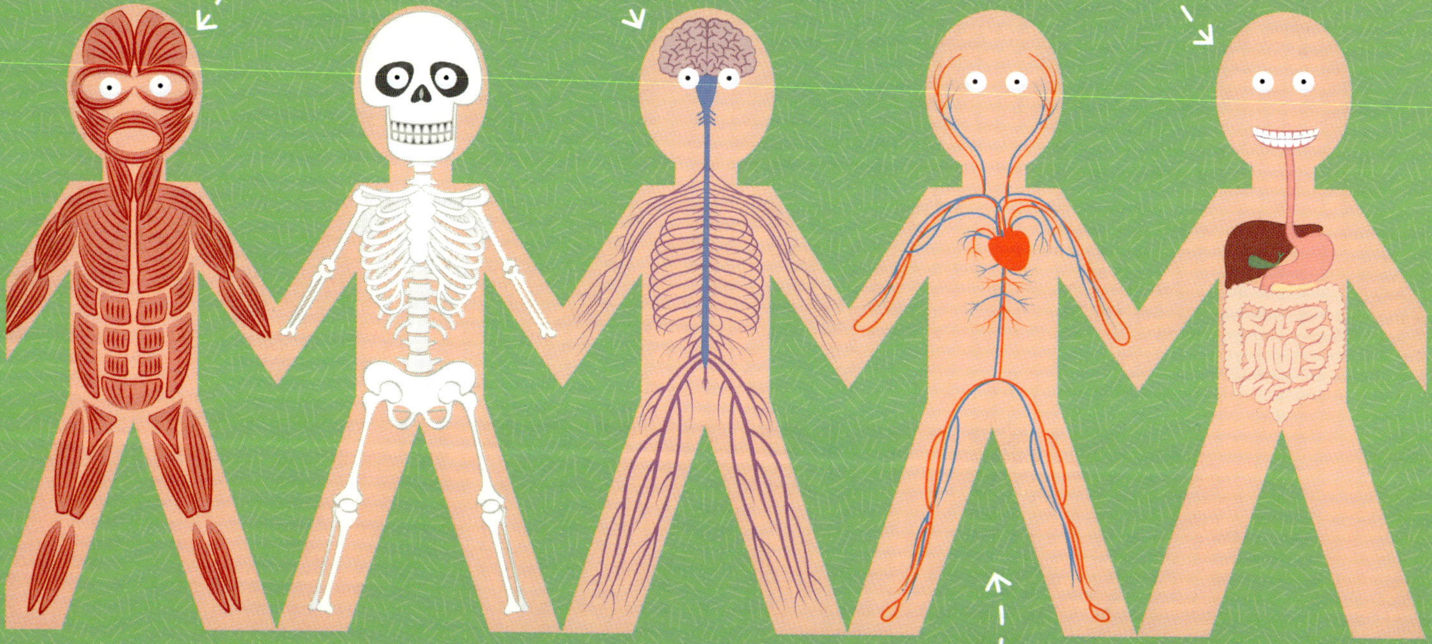

How does your body work?

Your body is all about teamwork. Different parts work together in teams, called systems, to perform different tasks.

What team is your brain on?

It's part of your nervous system, which is constantly at work, sending messages all around your body.

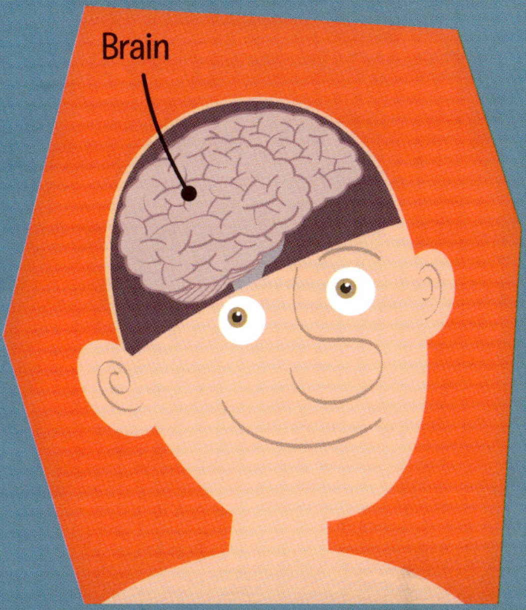

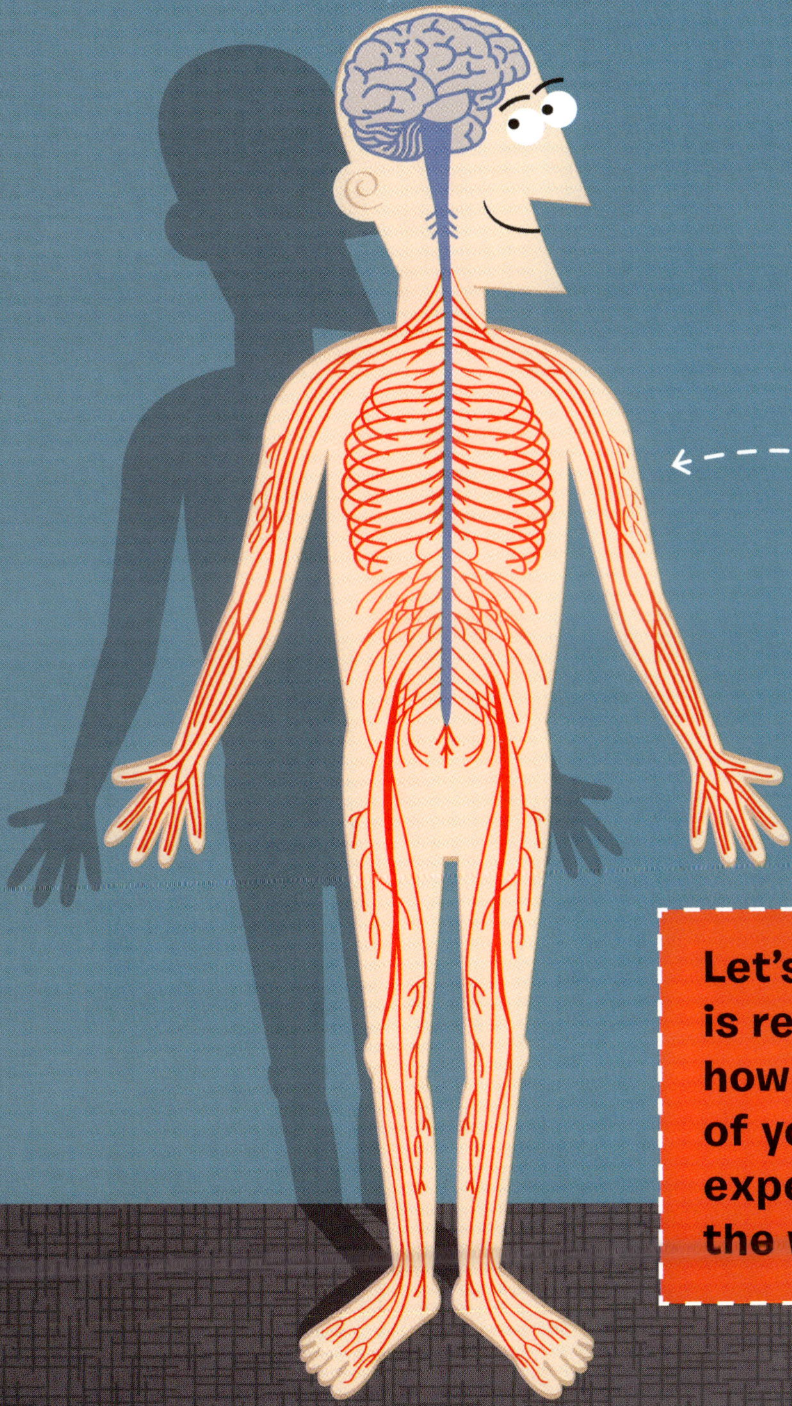

Let's find out what your brain is really capable of, and see how it works with the rest of your body to help you experience and interact with the world around you.

DO YOU MIND?

Inside your head is a supercomputer. It's called a brain, and it's always telling the rest of your body what to do.

What does your brain look like?

It looks like a big, squishy, wrinkled walnut. It's mostly made of fat and water. While not the prettiest organ, it is definitely the smartest!

How does it work?

Your brain is like a big messy bundle of wires. These wires are called brain cells, and you have 100 million of them!

They constantly zap messages to each other, making trillions of connections!

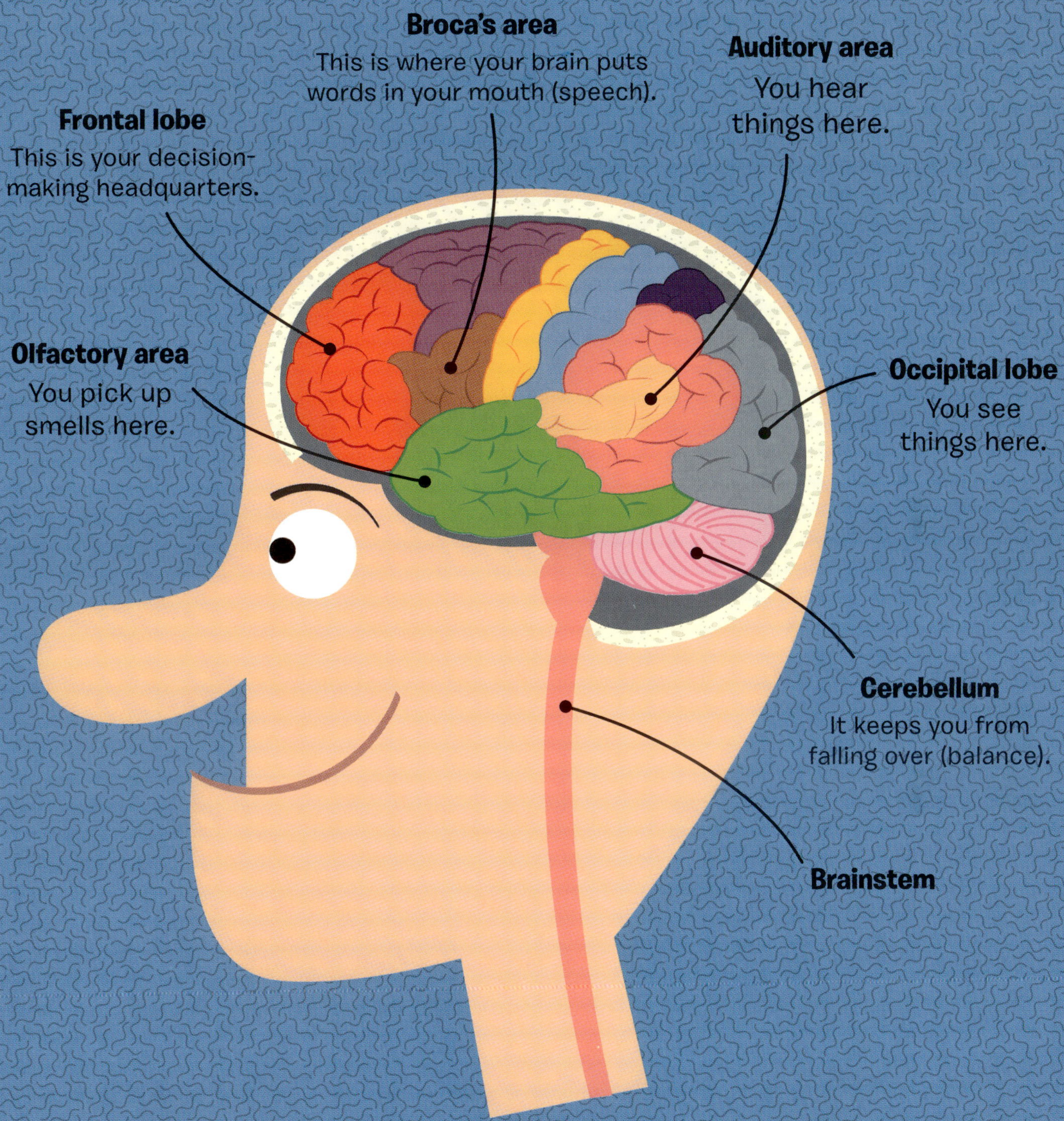

What goes on where?

Each part of your brain has its own job controlling what you do, from speaking to moving.

YOU'VE GOT A NERVE!

Our body has its own messaging system called nerves. They send information from every part of your body, and keep it all under control.

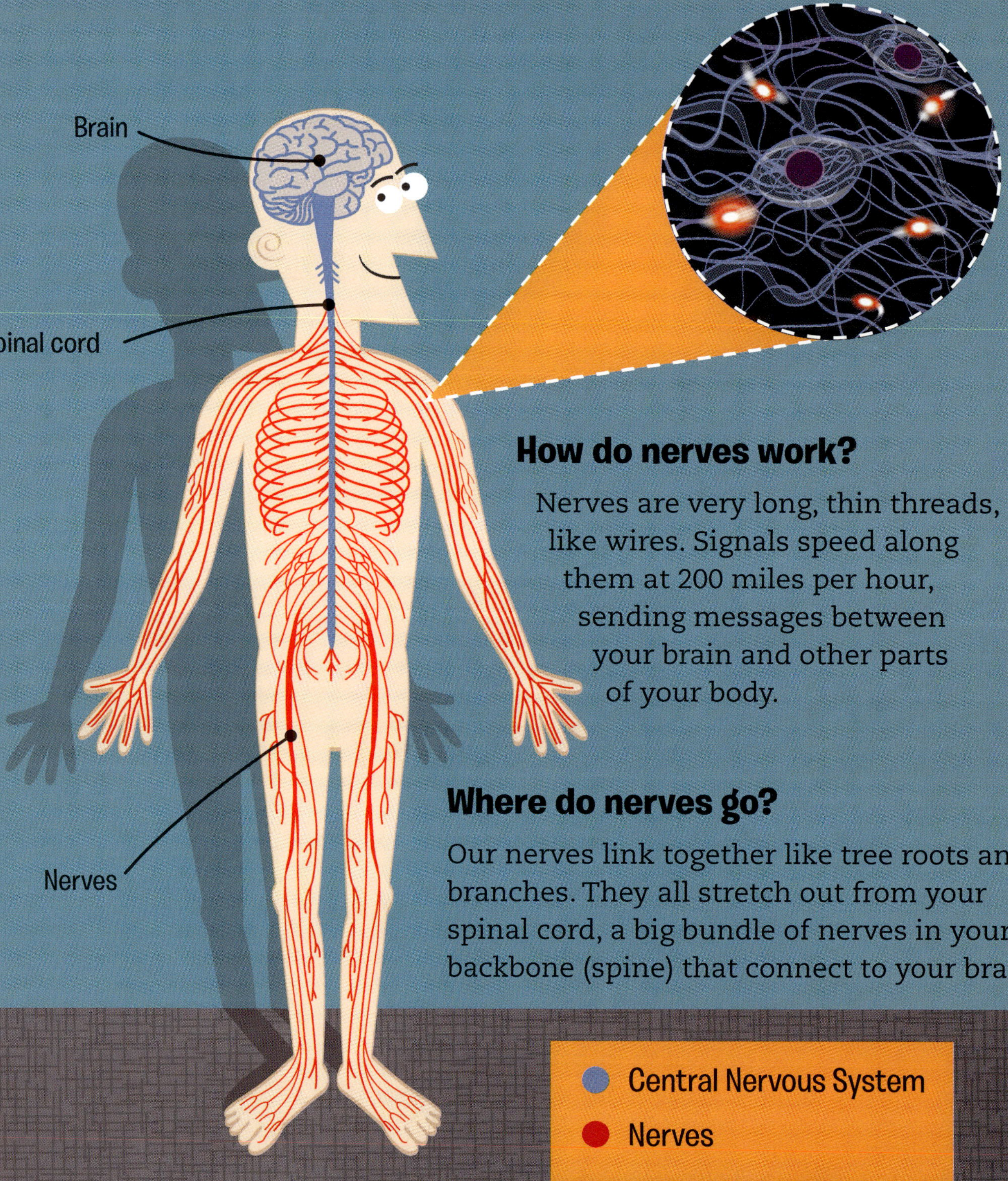

How do nerves work?

Nerves are very long, thin threads, like wires. Signals speed along them at 200 miles per hour, sending messages between your brain and other parts of your body.

Where do nerves go?

Our nerves link together like tree roots and branches. They all stretch out from your spinal cord, a big bundle of nerves in your backbone (spine) that connect to your brain.

Central Nervous System

Nerves

What's a nerve?

Nerves are made of special **cells**, called neurons. Messages to and from the brain are passed from one neuron to another, like in a relay race.

Receptors

Receptors in these branches pick up messages from other neurons.

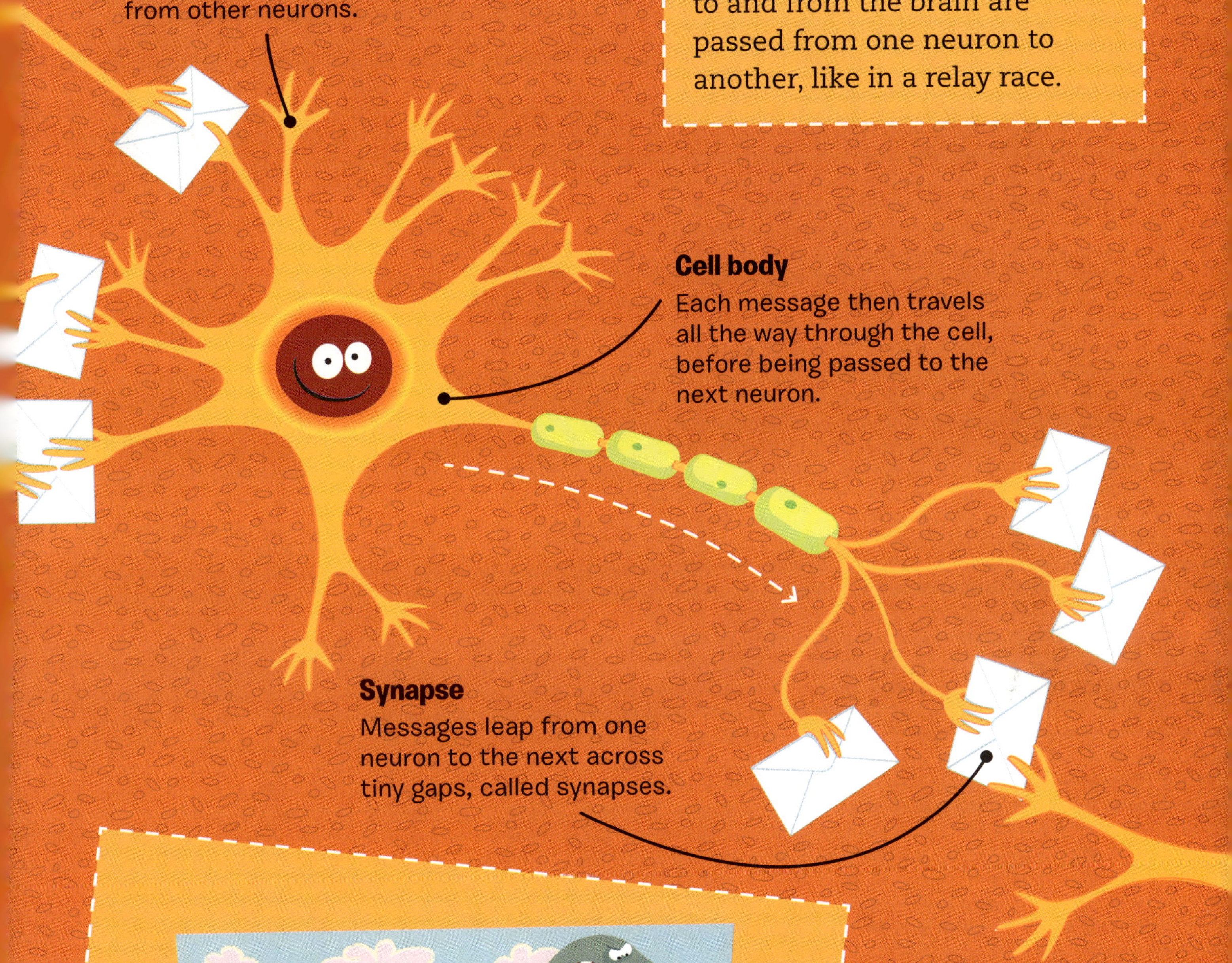

Cell body

Each message then travels all the way through the cell, before being passed to the next neuron.

Synapse

Messages leap from one neuron to the next across tiny gaps, called synapses.

How fast are your nerves?

Your brain can send a message for your feet to start running in just 12 **milliseconds**. Phew!

WHAT MEMORIES ARE MADE OF

When you remember something, a new set of nerve connections are made through your brain, called a memory trace.

How long do memories last?

Some things we forget at once, but some memories last a lifetime.

Short-term Memory

Some signals are forgotten at once. Others get passed to different parts of the brain for short-term use.

Sensory Memory

Your eyes, ears and other **senses** send signals nonstop to your brain.

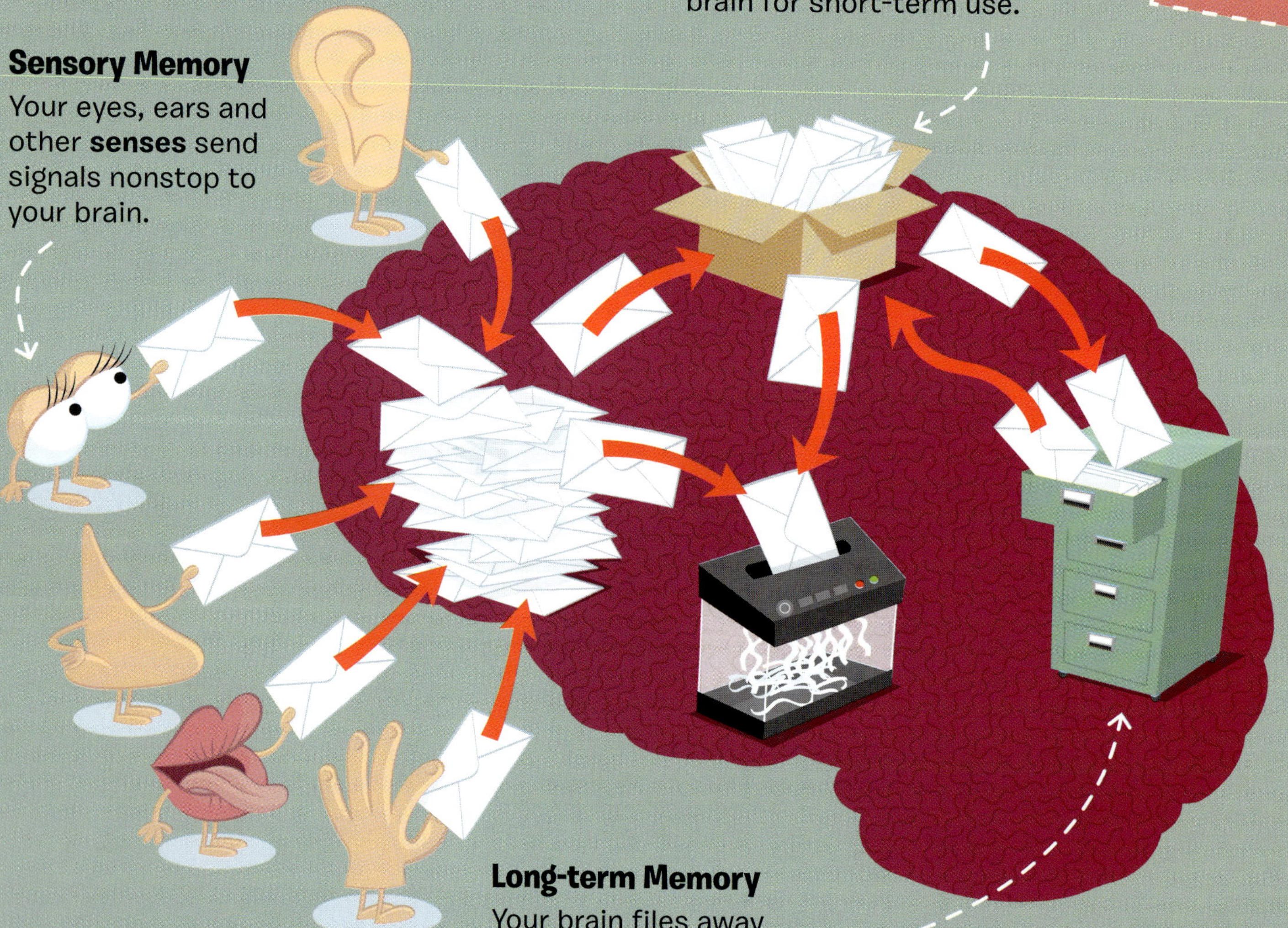

Long-term Memory

Your brain files away important memories by making lasting traces.

Do we remember everything the same way?

Some things you remember instantly, such as when you scored a winning goal. Experts call these explicit memories. Sometimes you have to go over things again and again, like learning a dance. These are implicit memories.

What's the world's tallest mountain?

It's Mount Everest. If you knew that, you're using your factual memory in the front left side of your brain.

FEEL IT! MOVE IT!

Have you ever wondered how your body knows when you touch things?

How do you feel touch?

Your skin is packed with feeling **sensors**, called nerve endings (because they are at the ends of your nerves).

They send signals through your sensory nerves to tell your brain what you're feeling.

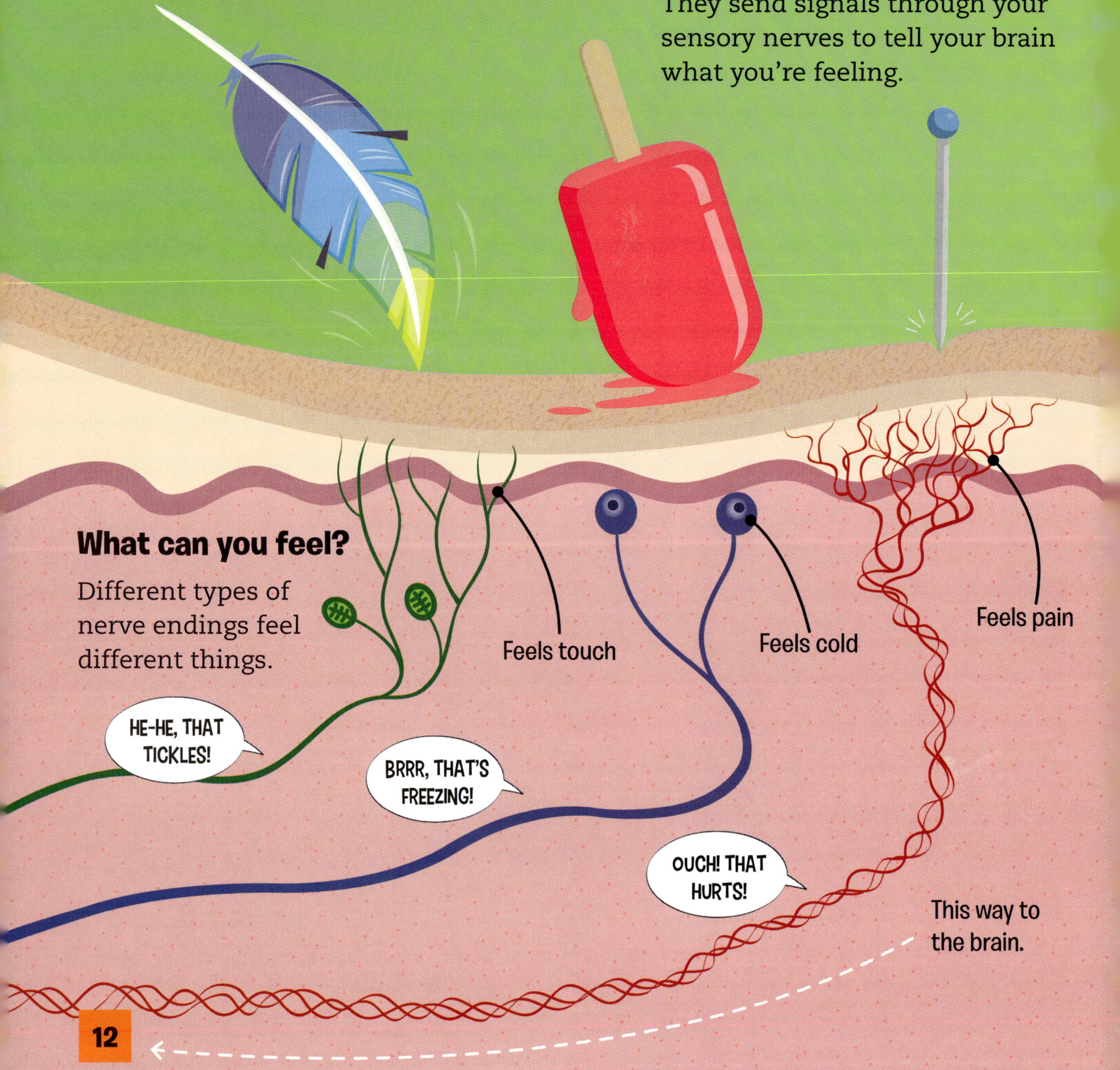

What can you feel?

Different types of nerve endings feel different things.

How do you move?

Your brain is connected to each of your **muscles** through nerves called motor nerves. When you think about moving, the brain sends signals to the right muscles to make it happen, just like when you stroke a cat.

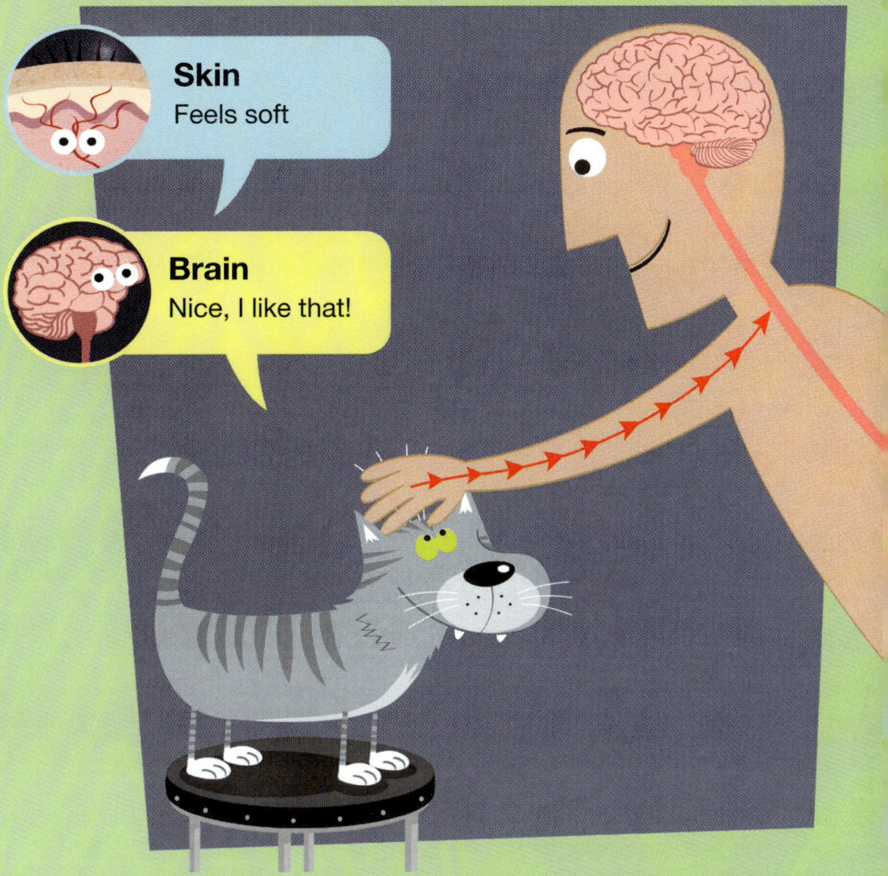

Motor Cortex

Sends out signals telling your body to move.

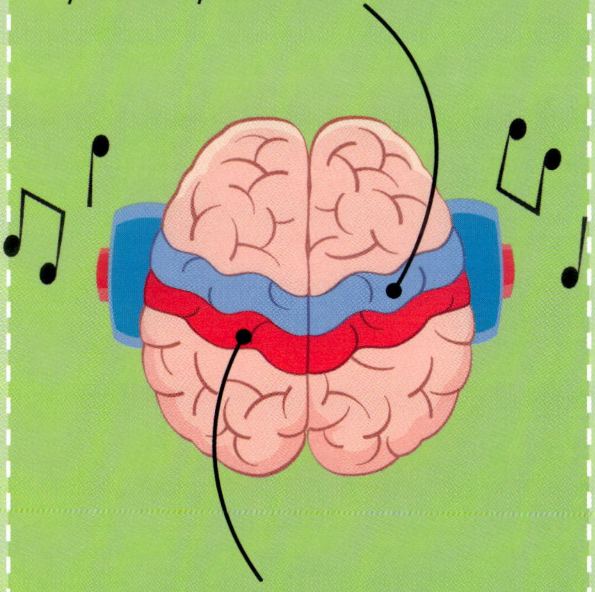

Sensory Cortex

Receives the sense signals from your body.

How do you control it all?

Your brain has two control panels across the top, in a band, like headphones.

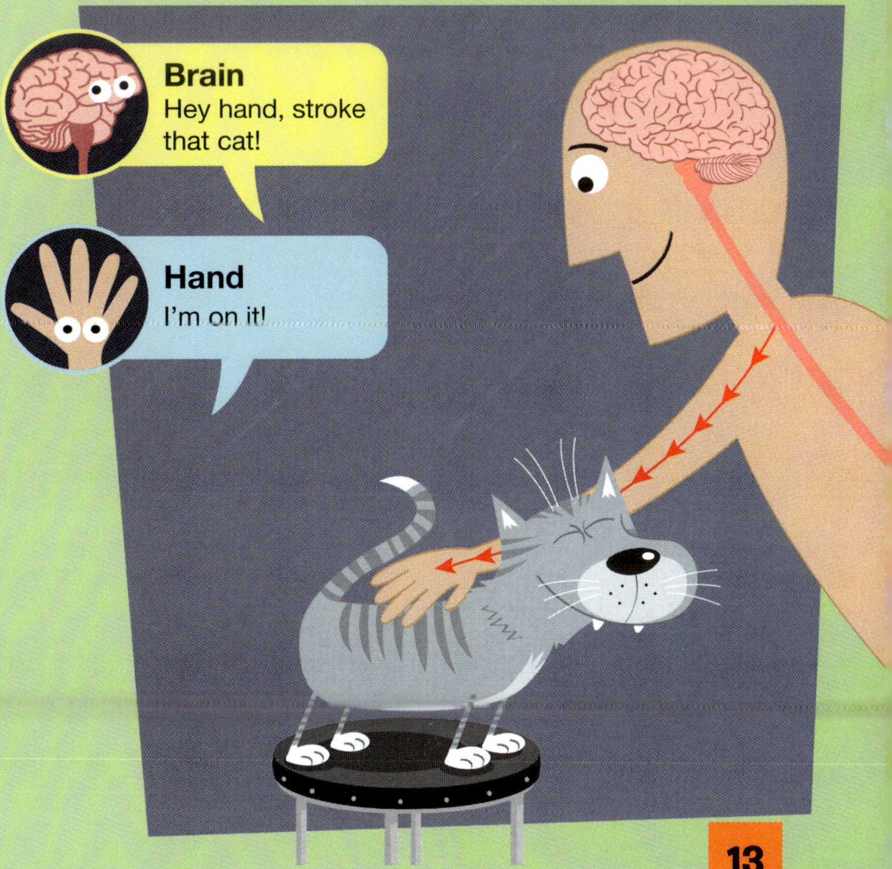

EYE SPY

When you open your eyes, you can see things. It's like turning on a TV. But how do your eyes actually work?

How do your eyes see?

Each of your eyes is an amazing personal ball-shaped movie camera.

Why do we have two eyes?

Try closing one eye at a time. See the difference?

Each eye gives you a slightly different view, which together help you see the world in 3D. With just one eye, everything would look like a cardboard cut-out.

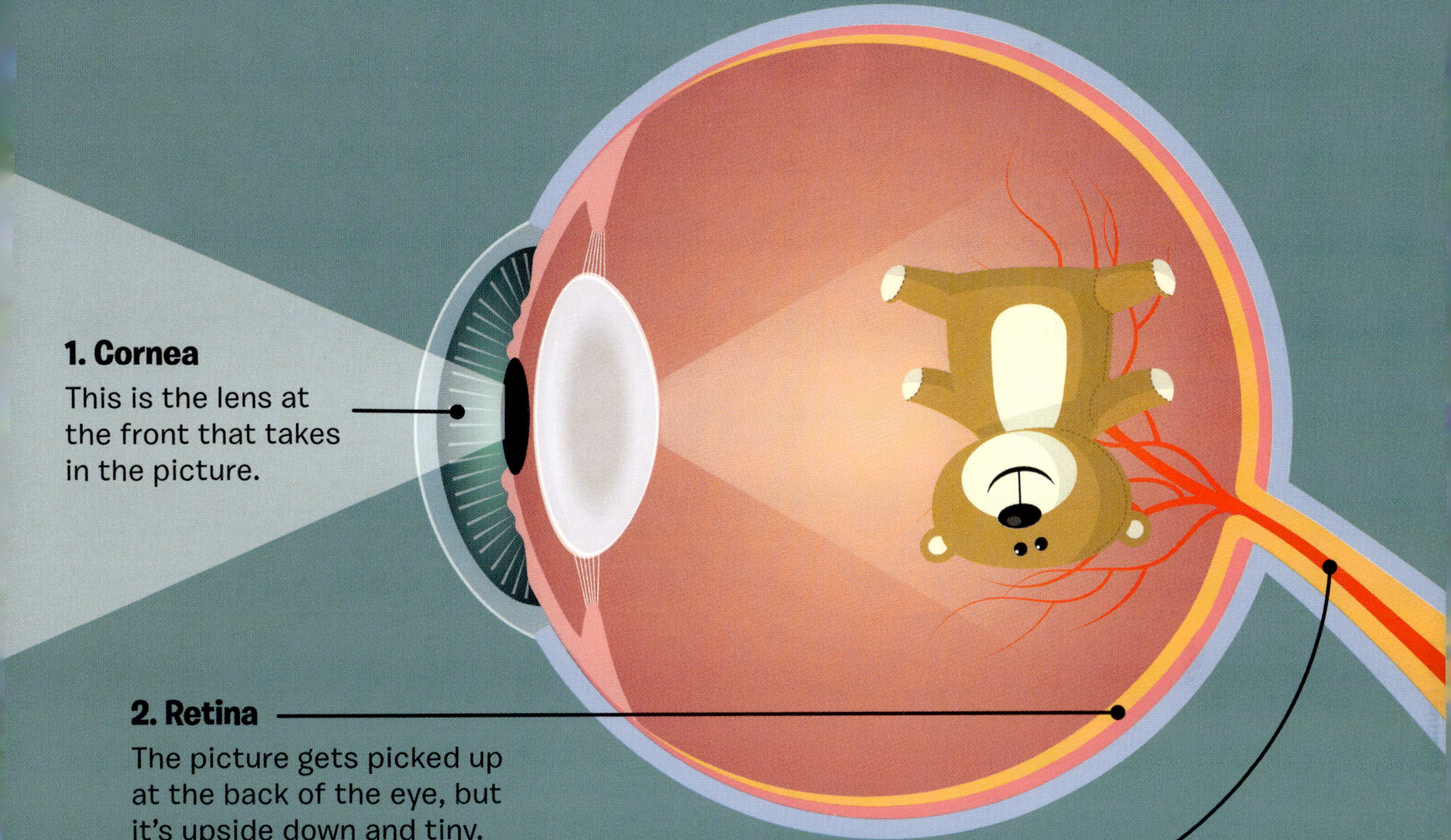

1. Cornea
This is the lens at the front that takes in the picture.

2. Retina
The picture gets picked up at the back of the eye, but it's upside down and tiny.

3. Optic Nerve
This nerve sends the picture to the brain, which flips it the right way up so you can see it as it is!

We have 200 eyelashes on each eyelid to protect our eyes from dust.

Why do you blink?

Blinking is when you open and shut your eyes so fast you hardly notice. You do it every few seconds to wipe your eyes clean.

I HEAR YOU

We hear sounds with our ears, but how do they do it?

What is sound?

Sound is the air **vibrating**. You may see the vibration starting when a guitar string twangs, but most vibrations are invisible.

How do ears work?

Ears are like trumpets in reverse. They funnel sounds onto sensors inside your head.

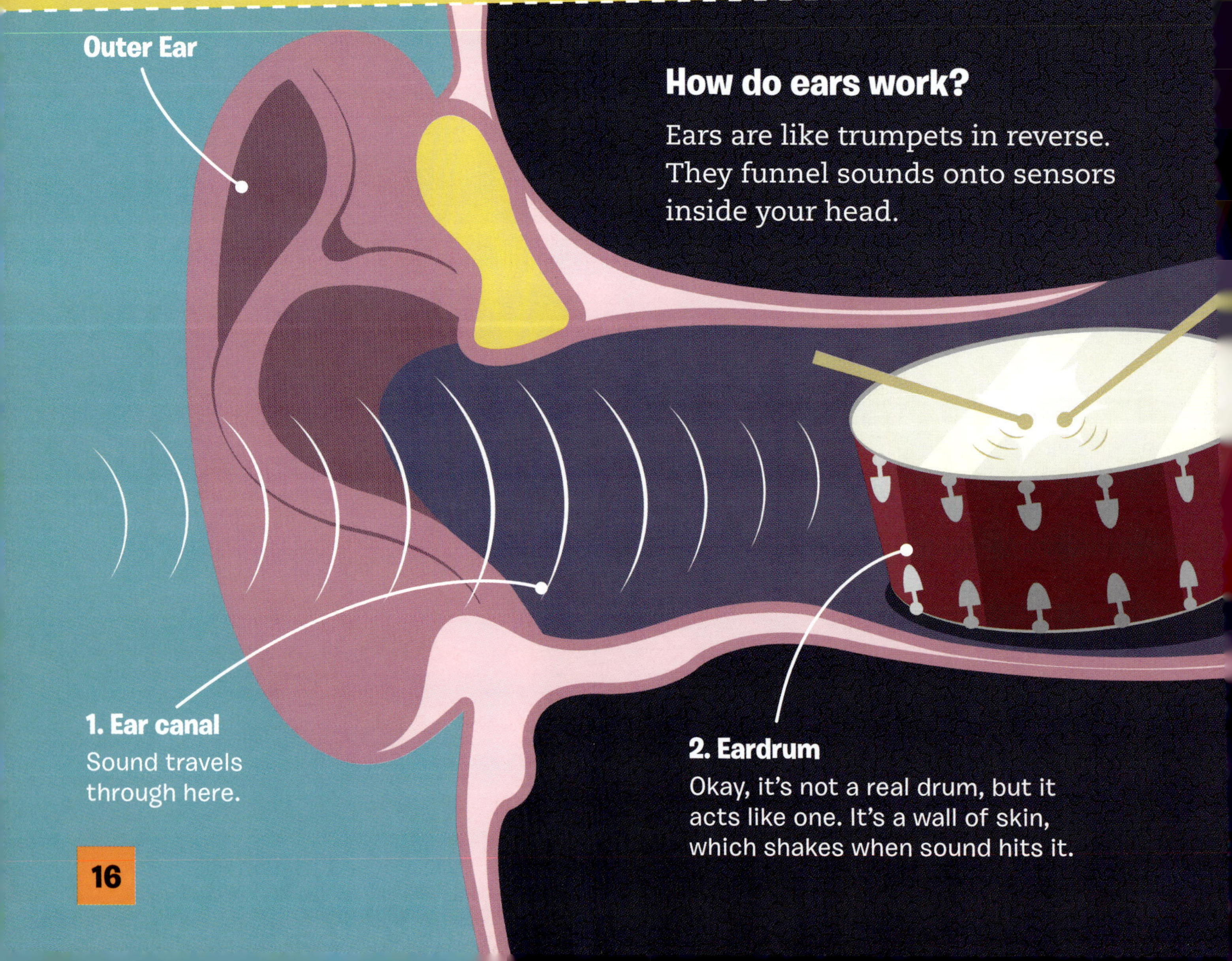

1. Ear canal
Sound travels through here.

2. Eardrum
Okay, it's not a real drum, but it acts like one. It's a wall of skin, which shakes when sound hits it.

Can you hear when you're asleep?

Yes. We have to shut our eyes to sleep, but our ears go on working. Our brain ignores sounds unless they are loud or sudden.

(This is exactly what your ear looks like, 100 percent. Okay, we may have exaggerated a little!)

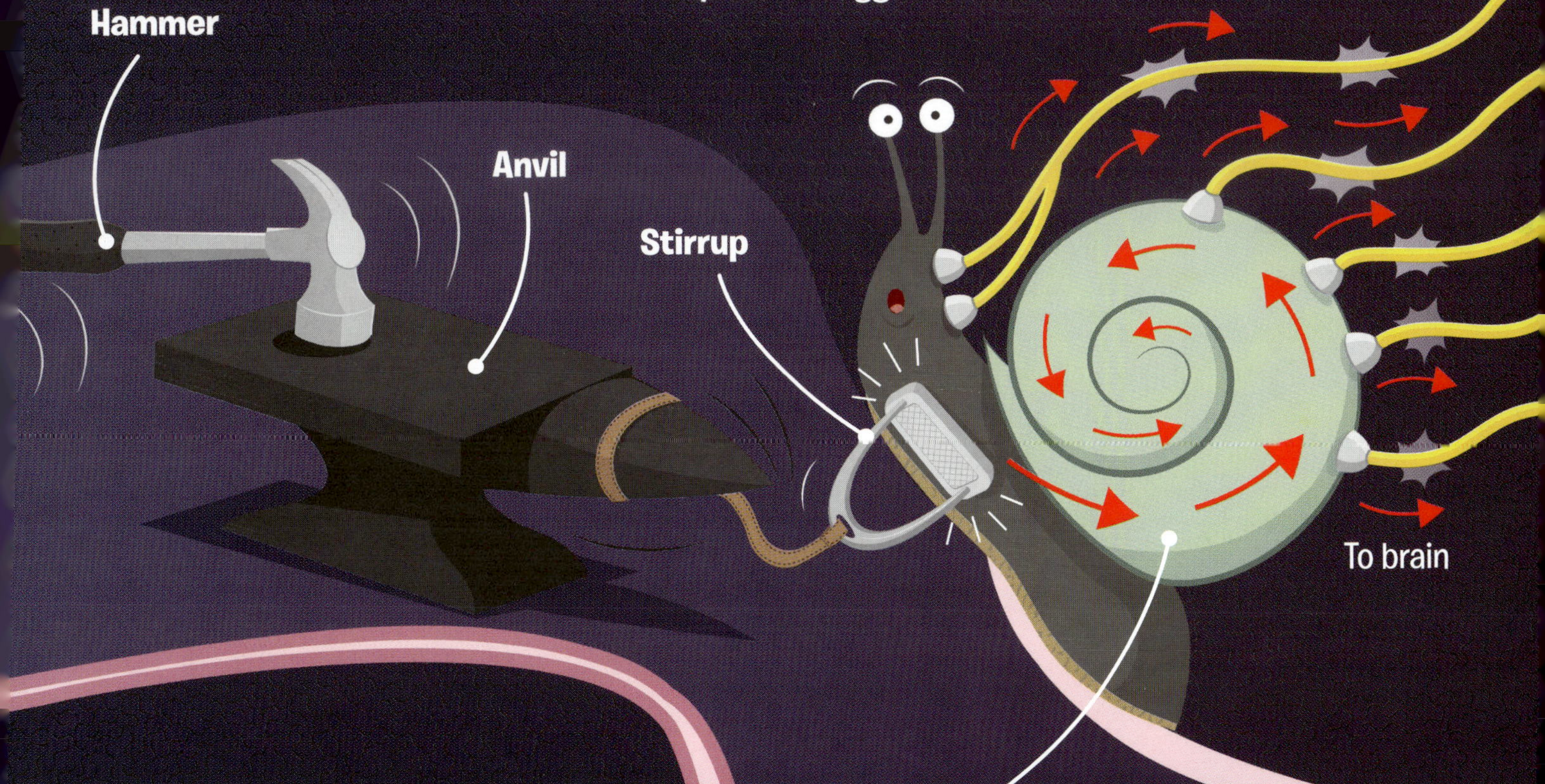

3. Ear bones

When sound shakes the drum, it rattles three bones, called the hammer, anvil and stirrup.

4. Cochlea

This looks like a snail and is filled with fluid. The rattling of the stirrup makes waves in the fluid that waggle tiny hairs, which send signals to the brain.

SMELLY AND TASTY

Smells get up your nose and tastes are on your tongue.

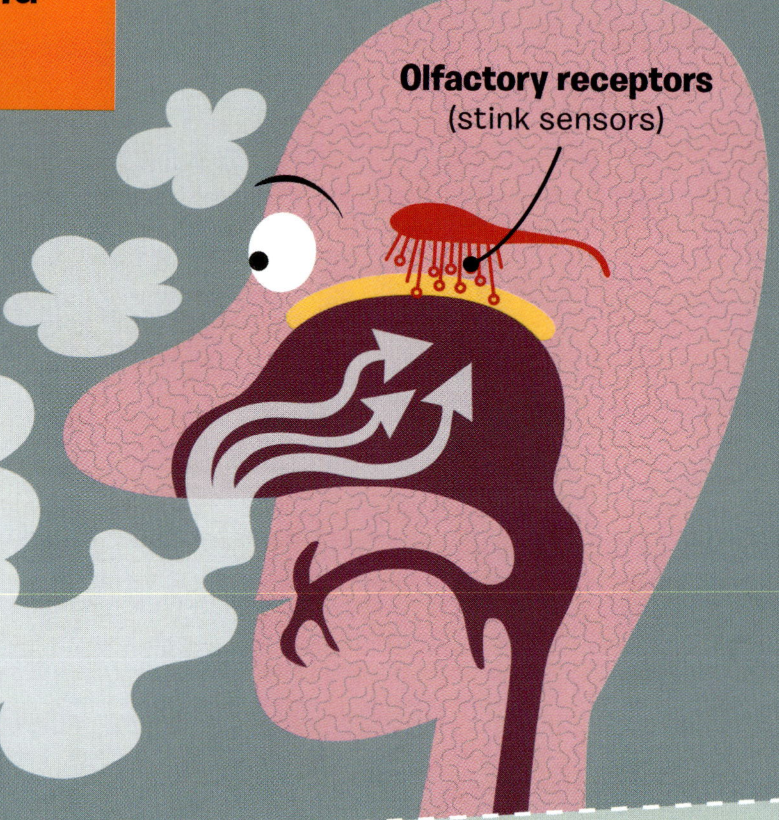

How do you smell?

The world is a very smelly place! Your nose can identify more than a trillion different smells with its bank of 350 kinds of stink sensors.

What can you smell?

Your nose is a super sensitive smell detector. In an Olympic swimming pool full of air, your nose could sniff a single stink droplet.

Do we taste with our tongues?

Yes, but that's only part of the story. Our tongues have thousands of taste sensors, called taste buds, but they can only tell if something is sweet, sour, salty, bitter, or savoury. We use our noses to identify the taste of individual foods.

What's the worst smell?

It's some scientists' job to make disgusting smells! Pamela Dalton made a stink bomb recipe for the U.S. military that may be the worst smell in the world. She mixed loads of gross smells together and called it Stench Soup.

SLEEPY TIME

I'm not tired at all! Why do I have to go to sleep?

Why do we sleep?

Scientists don't know for sure. They think it helps the brain recharge, like rebooting a computer.

NO SLEEP CHECKLIST:

- Your memory is terrible
- You can't think straight
- You get really moody
- You get wobbly on your feet
- You're more likely to have accidents
- You are more likely to get ill

What happens if you don't sleep enough?

A bad night's sleep just makes you tired and grumpy the next day. But a lot of nights without getting enough sleep will spell trouble!

What are dreams?

Dreams are stories and pictures that your brain makes up while you're asleep, like your very own private movie screening.

What happens when you go to sleep?

You go through the same four stages of sleep again and again during the night.

STAGE 1
1 to 5 minutes
You feel drowsy.

STAGE 2
5 to 60 minutes
Your brain slows and you sleep lightly.

STAGE 3
60 to 100 minutes
Your heart and breathing slow and you sleep very deeply.

STAGE 4
100 to 160 minutes
You dream a lot as your eyes flutter under the lids. This is called rapid eye movement (REM).

GLOSSARY

cells
Our bodies are made up of trillions of tiny, squishy packages, called cells. We have lots of different types of cells for each body part.

milliseconds
There are one thousand milliseconds in a second.

muscles
Muscles are parts of your body that tighten and relax to make you move. You have more that 650 muscles all over your body.

senses
Nerve endings that detect changes in the world around you or inside your body, including heat and light.

sensors
Something that picks up on certain physical things from the world around you, like heat, light, sound, taste and smell.

vibrating
Shaking, or moving back and forth (or up and down) very quickly.

INDEX

About the Author

John Farndon is the author of a huge number of books for adults and children on science, history and nature, including international bestsellers, *Do Not Open* and *Do You Think You're Clever?*. He has been shortlisted for the Young People's Science Book Prize five times, including for the book *Project Body*.

About the Illustrator

Alan Rowe has been working as a freelance Illustrator since 1985. His work is heavily influenced by 1950s and 60s cartoons. Maybe all that time spent glued to the TV as a child wasn't all wasted!